THE BORDERS POETRY ANTHOLOGY

First published in Scotland
in 1995
by
VA Publications Ltd

 This publication has been produced with
support from Scottish Borders Enterprise

Typeset by EMS Phototypesetting
Berwick upon Tweed

Printed by Martins The Printers, Spittal, Berwick upon Tweed

We are privileged to have secured the services and talents of Assunta Arrighi in the production of this anthology.

Assunta is well known throughout the Borders as an artist, poet, writer and photographer. Her work has made a substantial contribution to Art and Literature in the area.

The anthology has been made somewhat unique by Assunta enabling us to show a small selection of her art work and illustrations which thereby enhance this first Borders anthology.

Noted also is her undertaking of editing this publication for which we are indebted to her.

VA Publications Ltd.

FOREWORD

BORDERS ANTHOLOGY

The Borders Anthology is a collection of poetry written by people who have a special interest in the Border Lands past and present.

The poems included in this anthology show a diversity of emotions, pride and feelings by people who were not only born in the Borders but others too who came to make the Border Lands their home.

The Border Lands are steeped in history and heritage and have the most beautiful scenery, which is equal to anywhere in the world. For these reasons alone the Border Lands should not be forgotten.

Visitors and tourists who come to the Borders are intrigued by the beauty and history surrounding the Border Lands and invariably come back time and time again to sample what we Border folk have on our own doorstep.

Assunta Arrighi
Editor

CONTENTS

A Borderer

One who lives near a frontier

Borderland

A land contiguous to a frontier

The Borders

A stretch of country lying on both sides of the frontier

THE SPELL OF THE BORDERS

The Border casts a spell on me
And draws me North again
Its serpent roads and rounded hills
Invite me to remain

So it's North of Tyne to Carter Bar
The air so clean and sweet
There's gorse and broom and heather too
Beside my striding feet

Beneath the green hills solitude
Lie the silver secluded lochs
Fed by a host of little burns
That ripple past pebbles and rocks

The curlew pipes its haunting song
Recalling days forever gone
Of forays, feuds, and old romance
Of ruins, towers and battles won

Of trotting horses in the night
Fierce moss troopers on the reivers' road
Riding South to steal the cattle
Sword and shot their only code

Romance too and works of art
The Borders have much to recall
Sir Walter Scott loved what he saw
Bemersyde's views still there for all

Character shows in town and farm
Sturdy and honest and differently built
Stearner stuff than thatch and oak beam
Befitting the folk of the kilt

Melrose, Jedburgh, Selkirk and Duns
Douce grey towns with solid wall
And lovely names of rivers fair
Tweed, Esk, and sweet Yarrow call

To linger by their shady banks
To lift our eyes to hills above
Refreshes the mind and calms the soul
Where countries meet...I choose to roam

Norman Brewster

1

DEAR BORDERLANDS

Looking over to the Cheviots, I am looking to home
Which ever part of the Border I roam
For my kin came from each side of the hill
So I belong to each beautiful part
England and Scotland sing in my heart

At my work, two of my friends worked and shared the day
They are now dead, I still walk the way
I stand and look across at sunset's blood red sky
Remembering the foreign earth soaked in blood
Not enemies, but fighting side by side
To save the lands we love

Miriam S. Stamp

THE BORDER LANDS

Russet and yellow, the moorlands unroll
To cool verdant pastures, that gladden the soul
Rivers where yearly, the salmon will leap
While high on the hillside, graze... polka dot sheep

Yet the scars of the past are still there to be seen
Bearing wonderful witness to what once has been
Bold castles, proud abbeys with turbulent past
Skeletons, enduring and tranquil at last

This land of the Reiver and times that were hard
Inspiring the Artist, the Author, the Bard
For centuries despoiled, laid waste and in pain
Still wild and romantic...now at peace again

Anne E. Taylor

OVER THE BORDER

Like flame-shot smoke of ancient wars
The mists spill down the hills
To fill the air with crystal tears
That flood the tumbling rills

Amid the swirls of shadows shapes
Take forms of kilted men
With bonnets blue they swing along
And down the mountain glen

The winds that whisper in the trees
Disjointed echoes hold
Of men who fought the English foe
For Scotland of the bold

Then lifts the mist and flings the sun
Against the hirsels fleece
And just the crystal waters speak
Amid the hills of peace

Les Parsons

4

BETWIXED

I stand aware in no-man's land
but just at hand
To right, and left there stands
like meteorite
Two plinths of stone that show
the names of famous lands

I walk five paces South
and touch my England
And then ten paces North
and filled with pride
I stand beside
Scotland

The blood now racing in the mind
helps me to find the beauty of these lands
And Nature's power grants me a wish
To tell me clearly
what I am
British!

Douglas Haig Griffiths

5

BUCKHOLM HILL

Buckholm Hill, o' Buckholm Hill
I've roamed o'er you when all was still
I've jumped your brooks and climbed your stiles
And tramped your gorse for many miles

I've heard your larks in sweetest song
And dreamed my dreams with them so long
'Til startled by the grouse's call
It seemed the harshest sound of all

I loved you in my boyhood days
When I explored your many ways
I loved you then, I love you still
My one and only Buckholm Hill

George Crossan

(Written by the poet at twelve years of age in October 1918 after hearing that his father had been killed in France. He sought solace in Buckholm Hill where he held many happy memories of his father.)

HADRIAN'S WALL

Bleak horizons
Eerie winds
Blocks of stone
Centurions

Miles of forts
A.68,
Vindolanda
Country Fete
Come here on a windy day
You're blown over the hills to old Solway!

Tony Green

THE BORDERS

Your rolling hills and clouded steeps
And misty autumn mornings
Your dark ravines and upland peaks
And birdsong laden dawnings

Your heather scented moorland ways
And tinkling burns and streams
That flow from shadow into light
And shifting sunlight gleams

Your gracious oaks as old as time
And leafy forest groves
Tall grasses rippling line on line
Whene'r the west wind blows

Grey ruined towers and castles old
Still many a secret keeping
With watchful vigil on your heights
Through centuries unsleeping

And then the storms in winter break
And howling blizzards blow
And swoop upon your realm to shake
A coverlet of snow

On shimmering lakes, now grey, now light
On ancient woodland reaches
And rugged cliffs that brood upon
Your coves and seas and beaches

There wild tempestuous windblown waves
That roll without a pause
And gather strength to fling themselves
Upon your stony shores

Your changing aspects, dark and light
May you be tamed never
Though man may stay or man may die
Oh Borders...live forever!

Sybil Sibthorpe

8

THE NORTHERN BORDERS
MISCONCEPTION RECTIFIED

It is scarcely half a century
Since far North of this fair Isle
Was regarded by most Southerners
As dark and dreary, cold and wild

Love for a man, brought me North
In the year of Forty One
I packed my bags, prepared for the worst
Thought of as crazy by some

The wildness of the Border lands
captured my imagination
I fell in love with so much beauty
So I'm a Northerner, by adoption

For over fifty years now
I have enjoyed the thrill
Of introducing friends and kin
To every valley and hill

I've revelled in their amazement
As scenes of beauty met their eyes
Vast silent moors and wooded dells
Reduced the guests to rapturous sighs

I soaked their minds with local history
Regaled them with many a legend
As we drove, through valley and fell
Along the Roman road to Scotland

It was a pleasure to witness
The wide eyed admiration
When they viewed the Scottish moor
In all its aberration

I drove further across the Border
To show them the deep, deep lochs
Surrounded by valleys and mountains
Decorated with fringes of grey rugged rocks

An uncle from Essex...a wag of sorts
I can hear his laughing voice now
On his first sighting of a Highland beast
Exclaimed, 'Look, there's a hippy cow'

When they went home, our visitors
Said, 'The Borders are maligned'
Then described the wonders they'd seen
And misconception was rectified.

Marjorie Spark

9

A NEW BORDER BALLAD

The Border ballads sang a song
Of love and war and play
If those same Minstrels lived again
What would they sing today?

The cattle graze in peace and quiet
Beside the river bed
With no one to disturb their nights
The Reivers are all dead

True Thomas lay on Huntlie Bank
A ferlie did he see
No Queen of Elfland claims his heirs
Down by the Eildon Tree

For Ercildoune is Earlston now
With busy streets and square
Forgetting all the olden times
You'll find no ferlies there

But if you walk the Lammermoors
In wind and sun and rain
You know the past is with you still
You feel the ancient pain

And still the mists lie cold and chill
And freeze you to the marrow
As you pursue your lonely road
On the dowie dens o' Yarrow

And so the poets of today
Take up the ancient story
They sing the spirit of the land
Of love and loss and glory

Mercedes Claraso

10

WHY I LOVE THE BORDERS

A city slicker tae a Border toon
thought the'd never settle doon
From a rat race life...they were sorely torn
tae the bus no' comin' the day, but...maybe the morn!

A slowed life...the envy of most
but a way of life, I now would boast
Here...silver salmon leaping wild
on an angry Tweed when nature riled

Here in gay abandon, wild life roam
through luscious forests deep in loam
The Stately Homes to visit in number
sport ornate gardens...so full of wonder

Attentive Doctors ever ready to call
and caring Vets...on the ball
Not so far away there's sea and sand
with Tweedmills looming o'er virgin land

Farming, fishing, or game to order
all part of life that surrounds the Border
But most of all...I'll tarry a while
wie' friendly folk...who have time to smile!

Elizabeth Ann Hutchison

ENCHANTING GRETNA GREEN

The kirk at Gretna Green holds treasured memories
As graciously she tells an ancient story
A cottage nearby touched by Royal flavour
Hosted Charlie's vision of proud glory
The Young Pretender sought a place of shelter
Returning home from England in despair
I wonder if his mind was troubled greatly?
He may have knelt to offer fervent prayer

Let us now pay homage to The Smithy
Peals of laughter, love is in the air
Centuries of echoes mingle softly
Ghostly figures solomnly declare
Hands across the anvil...tightly clasped
Elopers crave a blessing quite unique
Quaint, romantic, past entwined with present
Enchanting old oak frames too proud to creak

Adorned with honour...walls which feel no shame
Many famous people passed this way
The Smithy cradles secrets warm and wonderous
Written vows contented to stay
Modern times have readjusted custom
The marriage room invites a lighter scene
But history edged with lace embraces lovers
The everlasting charm of Gretna Green

E. M. Shirley

THE BORDERLANDS

I want to visit
Kelso
Where my family
All began
My Mother told me
Stories
Of her Father
Tall and fair
With a dour Scottish nature
Which descended on
To me
I've seen pictures
Of his home
I know I'd like it too
Scotland's in my blood
It's calling out to me

More recently
My daughter, my one
And only girl, wed
Her handsome lover
Across the Border there
Not at famous
Gretna
Too popular by far
But Lockerbie
Known for its
Disaster
Before their wedding day
Driving on to
Moffatt
They sealed their wedded
Bliss

Now I've two
Grandchildren
Both dour, tall
And fair
One day we'll cross
The Border
To explore
Our Homeland there

Judy Smith

13

BERWICK SHORE

Crumbling cliffs roll down to sea
Footpaths gone that used to be
Where waters deep, a grave provide
But give up on the ebbing tide

Erosion eating at the land
Where there was grass
We now have sand

Perhaps in time we may all be
Whence we came...back in the sea
Time and tide, it seems to me
Will take good care of that

Alan Duggan

EYEMOUTH DAWN

The sun picks up the fronds of earth's grey mantle
Dispersing to some higher sphere, the dregs of early morn
And glittering, wakes the slumbering headland, stirring seas
Performs its daily miracle...and paints the season's dawn

The breeze that drifts from sea to drowsing bay
Exhales its briny tang across a waking land
Daylight dispels the formless greys of fitful nights
Restores its genial colours with a kind and healing hand

From harbour's haven seawards steams a smack
Sole challenger to front a hallowed, fickle foam
Compliant cargo bred to brook the daily dues
To reap the oceans harvest...and steer steady home

Whilst vigilant seabirds dog their foamy wake
And swoop to snatch their quarry's silvery store
Their urgent case, in mournful strangled cries they plead
Pick up the chorus from their rooftop peers ashore

From earth – to sea – to heaven – a jetstream trail
Migratory passage thro' a new washed, azure sky
Impassive bird, with here and now commercial tastes
To trendy terminii its jaded cargo fly

Inconstant traveller...linger yet awhile
The vain and venal world demands too fast a pace
We have to change...to live with Nature once again
And you may find a measured peace within this place

Christine Henderson

COLDINGHAM BEACH

Faded painted beach huts
Rock pools and crab
Seaweed and pebbles
Sandy spiked dunes

Sliding slipping white sand
Blue butterflies
Crashing waves, foaming seas
Children's voices

Flapping deckchair canvas
Shimmering blue sea
Bees buzzing, humming
Deep still pools

Ice cream drips in the cornet
Driftwood and shells
Long grass, dusty paths
Tide now coming in

Claudia Montague

Coldingham Beach

ABBEY ST. BATHANS

Picturesque village in the Lammermuir Hills
With colourful rhododendron display
The Bank End once famous for its Mill
Pleasant scenery to enjoy all the way

There is hunting, shooting and fishing too
Magnificent Mansion which is Victorian
Strafontane Mill...now a ruin, interest a few
Certainly plenty here...for a Historian

Restaurant is licensed, name plate 'The Riverside'
They serve food of the highest standard
Frequented it is...from far and wide
You park near river, then enjoy a walk landward

On bridge most unusual...because it swings
Another has a Ten Ton limit
Interesting corner...has 'Toot' on a sign
Remember your camera...to bring it

The English arrived with their Army
In the year Fifteen Forty Three
They destroyed the 12th Century Priory
Walls they left...incorporated in Church...you see

Visit this Church, look into every nook and cranny
In the east wall you can view
Historical evidence to the delight of many
Lies the sculpture of a former Prioress too

Not far away is 'Edin's Hall'
This broch last used in Roman Times
Nearly five feet high, the base wall
Certainly not advisable for climbs

Visitors come, time and time again
To visit the 'Abbey'...in 'Abbey glen'

Ella Linton

18

THE GORDON AIRMS

When the road up the Yarrae reaches the place
Where it crosses the yin frae Ettrick tae Traquair
Ye need little excuse tae make oot a case
Tae stop at the Gordon, the hostelry there

Gin ye're oot in the car or jist ha'en a walk
It's a guid place tae stop if ye're wanten yer tea
While in the front bar, there is a guid crack
A interestin place, ye can take it frae me

Built bie John Gordon aboot echteen hunder
A contractor maken the Berrybush track
Peyen money tae navvies, it is little wonder
He thoucht o' a way tae get maist o' it back

The Inn was built while the navvies quick learned
That 'tic' was advanced as they worked for their keep
They sin fund oot they owed mair than they earned
Bie the time the road got as fer as Hartleap

It was here Scott and Hogg met, and they pairted
The very last time on earth they wad meet
James Hogg, tho' auld was still lion-hearted
While Sir Walter was bent and unshair on his feet

What pleisurs they've bien thae twae men; what glory
They heaped on the Border bie the wecht o' their pen
They uplifted us aa bie their verse, sang and story
Oo never wul see twae sic men again

Walter Elliot

THE GORDON ARMS

SIR WALTER SCOTT AND THE ETTRICK SHEPHERD JAMES HOGG
MET AND PARTED FOR THE LAST TIME IN THIS INN.
IT WAS THE AUTUMN OF 1830

GALA

Gala is a friendly place
Carrying on at a slowed down pace
Lots of hills abound
All around this little town

Like an alcove in a beach
A little place that's hard to reach
More silent than a city
More alive than any town of pity

In the centre of the Scottish south
The border before England's mouth
Engulfs us in a world of despair
Where people don't really seem to care

A home away from home
Where across the hills we roam
Where mountains are tranquil
And the people are thankful

Sinead Mercer

BORDERLANDS

Peaceful and tranquil areas
where you are free to roam and explore
Where smoke filled air, hustle and bustle
are against nature's law

You can stroll and wander to your heart's content
Looking at the scenery, studying the wildlife
It has to be heaven sent

Where else can you find beauty and innocence
You visit for free, detached from rush hour life
A visit to the Borderlands
Surely does make sense

Derek Crowley

AROUND CHAPELHILL

The Borders – a padded cotton wool country of silence and softness
where one can breathe and listen to the simple sound
of bees going about their work.

The stillness of hazy blue, different from yon special green
that rests and soothes and slows me down
while others work hard.

It's not a tranquil place, really, when you see with clarity.
That land is tough, has to be husbanded
unless you are lazy – like some.

The trees, tho' are hanging limp – finished with amusing
childish breeze and its playful airs.
Resting for morrow's blow.

The cattle lowing mournfully – it's a long walk back
to the byre and their milky way
strains the udder.

The bull bellows its demand for service, roars
manfully for rough hairy maidens
to ease its strain.

The sheep, like people following the crowd; all
with their own distinctive bleatings
that mark them out, together.

The wind whispering to let me know it's there
saying – I can really whip up a storm
when you least expect it.

It's beautiful this place, like many others similar.
We have no claim to it all.
Just search a bit – around Chapelhill.

Eric D. Davidson

COUNTRY COLOUR

Mist in the valley just before dawn
A lonely shepherd watches his sheep
Crook in his hand, cloak tightly drawn
Flock gathered closely safe in their keep

Soft flowing meadows of lush green grass
Stretching away to the hillside
Broken by streams as they lazily pass
Through dips in the rocks where minnows hide

Golden brown bracken scorched by the sun
Rustling gently, blown by the breeze
A hawk hovers high watching a mouse run
Not reaching its goal, snatched away to the trees

Clover and daisies, cowslips and harebells
Colour and beauty they bring to the land
From mountain to valley, lowland and fells
The splendour of the country...is something quite grand

Janet Bell

NATURE'S WAY

The sparrow hawk rises on the thermal air
He spots his kill, he fixes his stare

Wings tucked in he falls like a dart
Adrenaline pumping as fast as his heart

The mouse it scatters through the weeds
One swoop it's dead...and the sparrow hawk feeds

Shaun McDowell

POSTCARDS

Chalky downs lap to the south
Thatch and clay tiles bed down the cottages
Horizontal timber folds shield
From the salty eastern wind

Settlers splayed to the north
Dramatic landscapes hide rich pickings
Snapshots of castles to cottages
Sandstone through limestone
Knitted to distinction
Thick walls withstand surly elements

Across Hadrian's Wall
Breath-taking pockets of delight
Crystal rivers thread into deep lochs
Celtic heroes haunt the imposing mountains
Castles and great houses ward off invaders
Roof and walls stand sturdy with granite

England and Scotland
Rich arrays of colour
Bewitching tapestries
Stretch from shore to shore

Joanna Ashwell

25

ON A LONELY MOOR

Grey stone ruins on a lonely moor
What tales of the past they could tell
Would they talk of steel bonnet'd raiders
or of brave men in battle who fell?

Would they tell you of times they were hungry
When their livestock was stolen in the night
and the sight of their burning houses
or their children crying out with fright?

Perhaps they would tell you of their happier times
although I think they would be few
when peace reigned in this Borderland
and there were no hoof prints...left in the dew

Now no jangling harness or clanking steel
no sword or dirk at hand
no bands of raiding horsemen
Now there is peace throughout this land

And as I stand among these grey stone ruins
with their echoes from the past
I felt for a moment...I knew these people
May they have their peace at last

Brian Ducker

AYTON...A MEMORY

A walk through woods
Trees dressed in green
Bluebells wavering in the breeze
A winding stream

Stepping stones, children at play
The echo of a distant bell
The birds, and bees, and butterflies
All help to make this perfect day

Evening falls and with it brings
A most fantastic sight
A sunset lighting up the sky
A blaze, a glow, a heavenly sight
In all its glory standing proud
A Castle steeped in history
A memory to stay with me

M. K. Winfield

THE COTTAGE RUINS

Walking through the countryside
On a still frosty wintry day
Where a few little birds did stir
Along the rugged hedgerow way

When I came upon a cottage ruin
all circled round by fir
There I stopped to pause awhile
To reflect upon its past
When stepping o'er its little stile
On the house my shadow cast

There my thoughts soon drifted far abeam
As I could imagine the happy family scene
With children playing around the floor
Two girls and two boys
Rendering shrieks of laughter
When enjoying their Christmas toys

The crackling of the fire logs
The cackling speckled hens
The barking of their two collie dogs
The father mending all the pens
The mother baking the griddle scones
A treat for her hungry few
And all their happy Christmas days
They will remember all life through

The voices in the whispering wind
Will never blow away
I can hear them singing through the trees
As if it were today
So when you see a cottage ruin
Just pause for a little while
And think of all its happy days
Remember it with a smile

H. S. Paterson

28

STEEPLES O' DUMFRIES

Steeples o' Dumfries are bonny
Standin' high abune the Toon
Ilka ane gies fowk sic pleesur
Sichteers flock frae a' aroon

Win' an' weather tak' their toll though
Time has dealt a cruel blaw!
Greyfriars an' St. Michaels tae
Folk are fearfu' lest they fa'!

Gracefu' spires there, soarin' Heavenwards
Noo in need o' builders' skill
Steeple Jacks clim' ever upwards
They hae tasks they maun fulfil

Doonhamers will gaze yince mair
On kirks restored tae former glory
Spires ascendin' safe, secure noo
Happy endin' tae the story.

Valerie Inglis

NO-MAN'S LAND
(A COACH JOURNEY BETWEEN MORPETH AND EDINBURGH)

A pillbox of resistance
has weathered Northumberland
since the time of Hitler and the Austin 7
It stares blindly out at
a field overrun by sheep
They have made tracks
across this No-Man's Land
and hung their woollen flags
on barbed wire fences
Crows strut singly
like unpaid sentries resorting to pillage
Molehills show signs
of an underground movement

An ambitious sun
makes a foolhardy incursion into winter
Establishing a fleeting foothold on the field
it sets light to the shivering stream
before the raincloud cavalry
gallops in to put pay
to all but their uniform grey

Jeremy L. Slater

THROUGH A PONY'S EARS

The Borders?
I saw them once
Between the ears
Of
A pony!

Twitching ears
Forever there
In front of me
An
Irritation!

That animal
Beknown as Sparky
Suitable name for
The
Contrary beast!

We travelled
Round Border hostels
For several days
Of
Discomfort!

Sparky liked
To roll around a
Bit too often
For
My liking!

And scenery?
Lovely Borders' scenery
Framed for me
By
Sparky's ears!

Mary Fawbert Wilson

MY SECRET GARDEN

I step through the creaky old door
That opens to my secret world
Everyday things are there no more
And my heart is a flag unfurled!

The roses fill the air with scent
As they stand in regal splendour
Whilst the apple tree, its branches bent
Forms part of the pretty bower

The path is bordered with salvia
Shining forth their scarlet hue
Whilst in the shade the hostas mingle
With delphiniums in shades of blue

Against the wall, the creepers cling
Like lovers in embrace
And sunflowers shining brightly sing
To the sun they turn their face

There is no place so beautiful
As this garden of my dreams
Where the grass is always green

Evelyn Swanston

THE ACORN BED

But not so simply, to lend an ear
For fear the frogs would know it
To find you in your resting place
They would then overthrow it

This dome so small with cup to hide
The strength, the forceful power
The oak of pride
Secured in earth, so strong to greet the hour

Great winds pursue another dawn
Not touching through the bracken
Sheltered so tight in Mother Earth
This miracle soon to happen

The thrusting leaves break through the soil
So damp and dark with ages
Perhaps a primrose here and there
This tree to grow in stages

Then soon one day this mighty oak
Will reproduce her glory
When acorns fall again so free
Enhancing every story

At last, at last, the day is here
To spread her leaves so fine
Her nest of acorns now secure
Will see the march of time

The ripeness bursts, the heaviness hangs
These elevating leaves
The thudding thudding to the ground
This sap of great oak trees!

June Maxwell

Country Cottage

A TOUCH OF NOSTALGIA

In your hand, a picture of a house
Like lots we have seen before
Stone walls, slate roof, a chimney stack
Two windows and a door

A simple cottage, it was home
To a family all scattered now
To a Mother in a well worn frock
And a Father who followed the plough
To the girls with dark brown shiny hair
And the boys in tacketted boots
Mid the laughter, fun and banter
It was here we laid our roots

But time with his crosive lust
As in all things, had his say
The little house no longer stands
The old folk have passed away
Still, the man with his bulldozer blade
Cannot the memories hide
And thoughts of childhood's happy days
Fill the heart with joy and pride

This is the house where I was born
Just seventy years ago
Where the potter's wheel of life and love
Made me the man you know

Bob Dalgleish

SILVER TWEED

Stately swans
On sea and weed
Grace the mouth of the River Tweed

Waves a-rolling
Seals a-bobbing
Eider floating
Round cavernous rock
Skua, plunder stock
From lesser flock
By the mouth of the River Tweed

Firm pier stone
Flat slabbed throne
Anglers poised
Bait, bag, rod
Many an hour they do toil
In refreshing breeze
Awaiting spoil
Near the mouth of the River Tweed

Braving the air
Many a pair
Tread the stone
To the lighthouse cone
Over the wall peer
Birdwatchers to see
All that is dear
On the mouth of the River Tweed

Salmon leap
From the deep
At the mouth of the River Tweed

Nora M. Davidson

36

TWEEDDALE

Along the Border Counties
The Tweed meanders on
The homeland of Sir Walter Scott
And adventures long agone

From Berwick to the Bield
From Tweedsmuir, Manor and Lyne
Sheep and clear streams
Through woodland do entwine

Battles raged and blood was shed
By fortresses – the same
Who watch the chasing of the ball
In the Hawick-Selkirk game

The Howffs bore witness to our sons
Of inns and resting places
And here indeed did Robert Burns
Enjoy his whisky chasers

The Paddy slacks and threading glen
Moorland, birds and flowers
Where cashmere sweaters and tweed suits
Were weaved in drystone towers

Galashiels, Peebles, Montrose, Moffat,
Jedburgh, Selkirk and Ballantyne
What magic names the Borders have
Where lived Holy Thomas the Rhyme

And so my dears, the journeys end
My forebears are akinning
The Tweeddale name lives on from here
And this was their beginning

Barrie Twaddle

CUMBRIA

To live in a part of the country so beautiful and green
Where cows, sheep and lakes galore, are everywhere to be seen
There's hills and mountains surrounding, with wildlife abounding
So life doesn't go at a frantic pace
Yes...Cumbria is a wonderful place

We moan and groan and grumble about everything under the sun
Because it takes a lifetime to get the smallest thing done
We'll never have high speed trains or motorways around
But at least we can hear the birds singing
Yes...Cumbria is just grand!

P.A.F.

COLESSIE STONE

(The Pictish Stone at Colessie which toppled in Oct. '94)

See him not across the fields
Approach by hedgerow and low lying wall, treading through mud
Wild wind stinging rain in our faces
The elementals are against us
Protecting their Stone

Behold the Stone, not so far
That has stood, so many years, so many storms
Sentinel for Lomond Hills
Now cast down on the ground
Lying low, beached on the earth

Warrior carved, on warrior stone
What can you do, now you lie flat
When once you strode from east to west
Signifying something constant
In a transient world

Mother Earth, your time has come, to claim back your stones
Your warriors, your protectors, your beacons for deeper knowledge
Man and woman...we are desecrating
Your nature...we have betrayed you
And so the stones lie down

The Museum people want to take your stones
To lock them up, analyse, categorise, sterilise
So your protectors are gone
We are no longer in touch, we no longer know
How to treat our Mother

What do we do? How can we know?
Could it be that it is as simple
As putting upright this warrior stone
To protect our hills, our valleys, our rivers, our streams
And then the blinding rain stops...Look! Look at the rainbow!

C. Manson

39

HILL VILLAGE

Descending red
Houses are spread
Pink pantiles all

Ascending green
Large trees are seen
Ten fathoms tall

Forget-me-not blue
The brook dimples through
With tinkling call

To wavering yellow
Corn in the mellow
Beyond stony wall

Warmest of black
Night gentles back
Its summery pall

But dazzling white
Snow shines stark bright
Through long winters' crawl

Tony Green

A WALK BY THE TWEED

How peacefully the river flows
Upon its own sweet way
With gentle murmurings as it goes
All on a cold grey day

Its wide flung banks are lined with trees
Like green cathedrals rising
In emerald coloured harmonies
Their sweetness realising

And casting their reflections on
Its shimmering dreaming face
To mingle all their colours in
Its silvers, blues and greys

A sudden shaft of sunshine bright
From sombre cloudbanks breaking
Sets golden darts of purest light
Along far reaches snaking

And all the wavelets gleam and glow
In changing light a-changing
And glimmer in a dazzling show
Like diamonds re-arranging

And there a fish the surface breaks
The slightest ripple making
And stirs the water as it leaps
A hovering mayfly taking

And here a flash of coloured light
A kingfisher goes fleeting
And quickly vanishes from sight
On fluttering wings abeating

The flowers wild along its banks
On sighing breezes sway
They cast their petals as in thanks
Along its lapping bay

To make a floating bridal path
A wondrous sight indeed
That lifts the soul and cheers the mind
While walking by The Tweed

Sybil Sibthorpe

41

DUNS

Duns, our pretty County Town
Say we...Birthplace of 'John Duns Scotus'
Another town, making this claim, is 'Down'
Of the philosopher...also known as 'Dr Subtilis'

Our own 'Jim Clark' Champion in racing
Visit New Town Street...see his trophies
Beautifully displayed in glass casing
In motor racing, a word for him...'Apotheosis'

Jim lost his life in Sixty Eight
Gone, but not forgotten
Sad for all, he met his fate
We still express...our lamentation

The 'Summer Festival' is nothing new
It lasts all week, every summer
This a must for visitors too
Who can visit 'Duns Law'...with the 'Reiver'

Abundance of shops and eating places
Other interesting places to visit
The County Show...see well known faces
No one likes to miss it

Proud we are, the Queen's been too
What an honour for us
So many people, come to see
This town, famous for...John Duns Scotus

Ella Linton

A NORTHERN TRAIN JOURNEY 4:47

At 4:47
The road is a river in spate
pouring towards the grey estuary
of the sodden sky

Familiar outlines blur beyond recognition
disfigured by the staining rain
Gloom oozes up out from the fields
blotting out reality with
its cauldron brew of
dark imaginings

Trees line the journey
like a mutinous retinue
of sculpted screams
the colour of death

This is the time to be
indoors, in the light
in the kitchen, in love

But no,
4:47 is the limbo
of the commuter soul

Jeremy L. Slater

LAAL NELLIE

When laal Jim left us so so quick
He should have left Peggy an old walking stick
But he left laal Nellie
It's a wonder she hasn't a pain in her belly

That laal sheep dog
Can chew her way through a six inch log
We've tried all sorts to save her shed
It's a wonder to me she ever wants fed

The wood and stones to keep her in
Peggy's hammered on lumps of tin
The only thing left is a muzzle
For Nellie the sheep dog puzzle

Grace Sloan

FEELINGS

What is this feeling
I cannot find
What is this feeling
Always on my mind

The hurt, the sorrow, the pain
Are the only things I gain
Not happiness, laughter or love
That I am always thinking of

What is this feeling
When my heart aches
What is this feeling
My heart makes

I long for that love
That everyone keeps talking of
To come and sweep me off my feet
But when, oh when...shall we meet?

Michelle Amanda Whiteley

TIMEPIECE

Time was, or is as infinite as Space
Not bounded by some limit which our senses try to see
Time mocks our souls
Its controversial face
Rejects our logic, confutes sure reality
Thus, so bemused
We strive and seek to find
Space – Time
Confused at once with Like and Kind

Space is or was as flexible as Time
Filled never, or forever, as our concept wills our view
Space calls our bluff; disputes that claim sublime
We mortals posture
That our reason makes it true
Still undeterred, we sift through abstract thought
Timeless, bereft, and left in doubt...with nought

So how in faith shall we resolve this task?
Beset by futile challenge
Whence beginning? Wherefore end?
Think well on this
That which we really ask
Confounds our judgement
What conceit we do expend
Sufficient space will need to pass that we
Know what God knows
So meantime...let it be

Ray Talus

46

TO AN EXPATRIATE SCOT

We could all write verse about Scotland's hearse:
Flodden, Culloden, the turn at Bannockburn
When cleared, off the kilt, off on roads that we built,
To Canadas, Americas, Australias, to 'Wha's like us?'

Then, with hearts and minds bought, and the battles all fought,
To look across oceans, with whisky-eyed notions
Of bens, and glens and proud way-back whens,
Of fathers called Mac, how you'd love to go back...

Would you see the young men sleeping in skips,
With Crisis Loan hopes engraved on tight lips,
The queueing with Platers, and Slaters and Caulkers,
And Welders, and Builders and sundry old Dockers?

Would you see the young mothers, their eyes set and hard,
Growing old as they wait for the next power-card,
With milk tokens traded, but jaded of view;
Would you ask yourself this: 'Wha's like who?'

S. E. Fox

47

A MARVEL OF NATURE'S CREATION

In seventeen hundred and forty six, history tells
Of nervous Weardale folk and how,
They mistakenly girded their loins for battle
Against two hundred Kyloe cows

It was the day of Charlie's defeat
And Border raids were rife
Many a life and sheep were lost
The Border torn by strife

With the news brought in from Culloden
And the raids, from North of the Border
It was excusable for these country folk
To see highland cattle, as marauders

Steeped in history, legends and mystery
Peace and tranquillity now abound
Grey, glistening and gritty, churches and castles
Sleepily stretch from hamlet to town

Soft valley dales, enclosed in high fells
Winding rivers that thunder, or murmur
Tree covered dells and vast silent moors
With a purple carpet in late summer

Cross over the Border, heading northwards
A wider horizon meets the eye
Valleys are rifts and fells become mountains
With awesome lochs close by

Vast moors and heather clad slopes
Meet in one glorious sweep
Open your mind's eye and you'll hear
The widows of Highlanders weep

The Northern Borders hold you fast
They fire your imagination
Once you have seen them, they never let go
A marvel of nature's creation!

Marjorie Spark

48

SHARING AND CARING

God has a special love for The Border Land
For it is enjoyed and visited by every race
Beautiful Scotland and England too, bounteous in grace
Hands clasp across the Border in faith

We honour and respect each Saint
For over hundreds of years, and dreadful deeds
We have learned to share and care for each needs

For Scotland the brave and England the fair
When standing together side by side, enemies beware
We will take on all who wish us harm
But visit our countries...therein lies the heart's balm

Miriam S. Stamp

POLLUTION

When the Border hills are fu' o' holes
O' the world's Uranium waste
When tatties are grewn on shunder fields
Wi' never a tate o' taste

When acid rain dreeps doon frae the sky
Despite ministerial doots
And sulphuric acid gauns tricklin' doon
Whaur yince was a routh o' troots

When the gowdspink coughs wi' waterin' een
On the brainch o' a deid thorn tree
What is the hope for the Borders then?

An there's less for you an me!

Walter Elliot

OUR LIFETIME

There is a world within a world
The one we understand
It holds so tight around us
It is like an iron band

It keeps us safe and warm
All trouble kept at bay
Until the wondrous moment
We see the light of day

Our new world is so different
From that we knew before
It broadens our horizon
Like the opening of a door

We see green hills around us
The blue skies up above
But still we feel a calling
Of trusting mother love

In life we reach maturity
With time still on our side
But then the years go faster
Just like a running tide

Our time is nearly over
Like a terminating lease
So all we have to wait for
Is tranquillity and peace

Thomas M. Calvert

MY LOVE

I had this love
A gift, a treasure
Taken for granted
To last forever

Then one day I awoke
My love had flown
Out into space
I was alone

Why did it happen?
Especially to me
Without my love
I cannot be

Olive Young

THE OLD TREE

Every year the old tree blossoms
And preaches resurrection
Once more I see with happy tears
Its ever new perfection
It has returned from wintry death, the dark I so much fear
The old tree which blooms in the valley every year

Its blossoms offer light and warmth
And it alone can help
When I am numb and frozen
And lost in endless night
It brings me warmth and hope once more after the winter storm
The apple tree so old and gnarled but yet again reborn

In days of sorrow it gives me strength
My never ailing friend
What comfort that its roots hold firm
And steady to the end
For though I was in darkness yet now my heart can sing
When the old tree blossoms in the valley every spring

Jeanna Holl

DEATH OF A MINE

The pit head stands still
no sound...only the wind
that blows through the empty shaft
What I wonder
would the ghosts of yesteryear
make of the death of a mine

The Steel Works are gone
no furnaces, no flash of blade
A town dies...the worker despairs
How I wonder
can this severed limb
be cast aside to wither

The Shipyards stand in silence
where the greatest ships were built
the skill of a nation
left without a cause
Why I wonder
is our pride allowed to die?

Evelyn Swanston

THE SNOWDROP

Drifts of white, but not of snow
in Border woods just now
Galanthus, beautifully grow
beneath the branch and bough

So small and white, and tipped with green
brave little soldiers in a band
fighting the wintry winds so keen
undaunted, fragile...there they stand

Ana Maria Dodds

DOGS AND FRIENDS UNWET

Rain –
Lashing, seeping, soaking, numbing – nearly horizontally
driving itself across the cowering green, unmercifully.

Puddles –
Unmoving, reflecting, rippling, bouncing – all alone,
all joined by trickling mud and dripping stone.

Clouds –
Hurrying, rushing, scurrying – hiding clear sky behind,
a quick, brief glimpse of blue, then covered blind.

Sheets –
Washing straight across, squelching slopes of sodden grass,
allowing no respite for shepherd lass.

Wind –
Gusting, moaning, disturbing, bending – anywhere to blow
its strength – to put on show.

Unwet –
Comfortable, cosy, dry me – inside a home
of warmth and friends – open to some.

Dogs –
Sniffing, licking, cuddling, snoozing – all tell tales
of wagging ends and welcomes from gales.

Inside –
And outside, here and there, now and then – no streets
of rain and puddles and clouds and sheets.

Just dogs and friends unwet –
no wind.

Eric D. Davidson

SPRING IN THE BORDERS

The Cheviot Hills are crooned wi snaw
But nearer the Tweed the welcome thaw
Has swept the furr's wi whetted blaw
An left them doubly rich

Yet aa the braes that norward face
Retain the mantle, laith tae chase
Wi winter's stubborn sullen trace
Skulkin in mony a ditch

Still, only crooned the hills wi snaw
As in-by daffies nod an blaw
Aping the wee bit snowdrops braw
An nature's aa atwitch

Yon lintie twitterin on the bough
Is halfway through his coortin now
He's busy sackin knowe an howe
O wool an moss an feather

The burns, ice bound the winter through
Have aa been mute, but now anew
They're murmurin an chucklin tae
The listenin reeds an heather

Now anxious wifie dinna fear
An dinna get in sich a steer
Your plumin's safe anither year
We're due some cantie weather!

Jock Dalgleish

THE BORDER WINDS

The Lammermuirs in heather bloom
while the Cheviots touch the sky
salmon leap in the famous Tweed
unless the river's dry

But the wind blows cold in our Border land
and many a plant life wilt
from where does it come...or where does it go?
Ye'll know...if you're wearing the kilt!

But wind or not...the snowdrops peep
and light to the soil they bring
arising from a winter's sleep
as if to say...'it's Spring'

Toiling Border wind and rain
even blossoming in the snow
in tune to a soft and sweet refrain
their petals seem to flow

Elizabeth Ann Hutchison

SACRIFICIAL HYMN

Many, groping in the early mists of time, had lost their way
Froze and crouched in dripping caves and eaten bark
Until a later people in the dawning hour
Found their bones in shadows strange and dark
Others, because their words were fire, were burnt...
They probed too deep, too much of truth they learnt
Or were crushed by jealous ignorance of human beasts
Lusting after martyrs' blood like gluttons at a feast

Many, oh many more, will still be lost:
This is no earthly play, it is an alien game
Proud nations are cast down and kingdoms pay the cost
Of war, where towns are eaten up by flame;
Great armies crushed like fragile cups of clay
The blood of youth in dark earth soaks away
And there can be no peace upon this Earth
Until the seeds of peace give new humanity's birth

Jeanna Holl

COUNTRY LIFE

Hard sullen soil, resisting man's endeavour
Gaining strength from winter's ice and snow
Bleak landscape, cold, unwelcoming
Is Nature always cruel?

Farmer watches signs of Spring awakening
Sows seeds...in hope of just reward
Receptive earth softens, welcomes nourishment
The cycle starts once more

Sun, rain, and wind, they need them all
To nourish, temper and develop
That growing bounty deep in Nature's breast
Will yield its fruit in due course of time

Man's livelihood entwined so close with Nature's plan
Rural life, distinct from city's bustle
Finds fulfilment in waving fields of corn and wheat
Reaps glorious harvest, rich and full

Julia O'Donnell

JUST SEND A BORDER ROSE

Tell me you are coming home my love,
Without words written or said.
Just send me a rose my love,
Let it be white or red.
White for love will do for now,
Red for passion later.
No need for words, written or said,
We shall not wait 'til we are wed.
Just send a rose.

Sheila D. Whysall

SEASONS

I love the feel of Autumn
When leaves fall off the trees
Gold and orange flashes falling
Down, down

The crunch of leaves underfoot
To get blown and trampled
By weather and wanderers
Kids' happy faces walking home from school

As the winter chill comes upon us
We shiver in our homes
Ice like glass
Snow deep as an ocean

White tipped hills
Fir trees abound
Waiting to be chopped
When Christmas comes around

The whole world seems to disappear
Until February the next year
Refreshed and revitalised
The world alive again

Sinead Mercer

ON DAYS LIKE THIS

Dark storm clouds gather, menacing the chequered
landscape below
Majestic mountains reaching skywards, taking in the first drops
of icy rain
In the valley, a lone figure lifts his head
Pervaying the darkening heavens that are changing
so dramatically
He shudders, and pulls his hood tighter around his face
As the first crack of thunder pierces the silence
Reverberating off the craggy rock that surrounds him

Frozen droplets sting his weathered face as through
shuttered eyes
A familiar sight is silhouetted on the horizon by a single
shaft of light
Which cuts through the inky skies like a shining sword

Home where the amber glow spills from the leaded windows
into the wet courtyard below
A welcoming fireside awaits behind the weather beaten door
which had seen so many days like this
Then, looking to his feet, his faithful fell companion
reminds him of duties unfinished
As the farmer and his dog resume their daily journey,
he knows too well
The welcoming fireside will have to wait

Pat Atkinson

WINTER MANOEUVRES

Wind bombarding the chimney stack
Hail gunning on the pane
Winter's ruthless army is on the march again

Platoons of scalloped snow clouds
Are hid beyond the hill
Awaiting further orders
To go in for the kill

Irene Wood

WINTERTIME

Now winter grips with iron hand, and frost lays thick upon
the land
And, from human hibernation, pulling hats to cover ears
Of people...old in years
Come all the glovey bodies
Folding scarves in coats held fast, 'gainst Jack's icy blast
And they go about their business in a hurry
Just as fast as they can scurry
And clumsy hands, encased in wool
Fumble for their change
In shops decked out with Christmas range

And soon the sky grows grey with flighting snow
And Cheviot's pale hills sparkle in the morning's weakling glow
Of pale sunlight, lifting leaden sky from long night's chilly rest
Casting its feeble warmth, sparingly
With grudging, athritic hand
And sleet and glistening ice prevail
But still leave room for diamond hail
Rattling loudly on the rooftop, and stinging face
As the Tweed moves on at a sluggish pace
Trickling frozen fingers into patches
Deep, sullen, at this time of year
As waste and debris catches

Then, swollen, bursting, flowing quickly now
Over ground where fill-dyke wetness lays and, rigid to attention
Stand the trees, bereft of leaves, by scything, cutting winds
Holding out their branches in delicate, lacery tracery
Where birds, their scaly claws clutched tight, sit, fluffed
Dull eyed, with heart beat slow, drizzled beaks muted,
without song
And timid deer come near, forgetting fear of man
For hunger pangs are strong
The earth lies hard and still, it waits, and holds its breath
And some things will be touched by the dark, silent, cloak
Of Death

Rosalyn Brown-Scott

65

BORDER SUMMER

Rise, shake off sleep...full awake to a summer's day
to live again God's gift of life
Watch the trees in a soft breeze sway
bask in the glory of a warm sun ray
forgetting worries and strife

Walk across the dew kissed grass
see the beauty of the Borderland
as overhead singing birds pass
Over yonder hill a colourful mass
of flowers...painted by a divine hand

Rolling hills and tall leafy trees abound
streams babbling softly as they go their way
To know marvellous beauty for miles surrounds
this hallowed Border country...world of many sights and sounds
Summer, on a quiet sunny day

To watch the sun sink slowly down
and listen, that mournful song of the curlew's cry
The heavens glowing like a scarlet crown
as Nature dons her soft nightgown
To know of another glorious day passed by

Climb a hill of verdant life so green
reaching the top to gaze down upon a valley deep
Nothing is more lovely to be seen
This Border world of beauty...has Nature for a queen
and though night falls...she works her magic while we sleep

Ron Davis

A CHANGING PICTURE

I got up so early in the morning
That it seemed the world belonged to me
There was a low-lying mist across the land
Just like a milky sea

The air was clear, and sweetly scented
There wasn't a sound to be heard
I got up so early in the morning
That I was the early bird

I sat alone for quite some time
Being part of the picture I could see
It was such a beautiful feeling
That the Lord had included me

I was lost in time, with my thoughts
Then the mist began to lift
And slowly, unfolding there before me
Was one of His greatest gifts

Here was a panoramic view of the Cheviot Hills
With mighty 'Cheviot' standing there
An inheritance to all Northumbrians
But a gift that we can share

With each passing of the seasons
A changing picture is there for me
But the real wonder of this picture
Is that it's there for all to see!

Brian Ducker

THE SWEET MELLOW YEARS

The sweet mellow years stay close to my heart
As the season of Autumn is nigh
Those Galloway Hills are clear in my mind
My breast heaves a wild aching sigh

A rainbow of love embraces my soul
To cradle my dear sacred land
My Autumn has dawned with timeless effect
I wonder was this, what God had planned?

Dark shades of Winter now threaten my view
As life's final chapter begins
Soon the Spring turned into Summer and then
The great race..which nobody wins

But blessed tho' I be with memories of youth
When the melody hauntingly nears
Those Galloway Hills enhance my last wish
To pause with the sweet mellow years

E. M. Shirley

THINK

A sea of corn swaying in the sun
Lambs jumping around having fun
Chicks in a nest high up in a tree
These are the things that please me

Bright perfumed flowers abound
Where else can all this be found
Grey clouds come to season with rain
Helping the land to live once again

The rose buds open as bees come and go
The performance of life a wonder to know
The world turns on as the days ebb and flow
As Mother Nature puts on her vivid show

Giving her kisses and love to the land
Offering all mankind a helping hand
Standing us food and warmth and drink
But will mankind ever stop to think

In return for her gifts we kill the earth
Never stopping to think of its real worth
Can we all go on destroying this way?
Will we all live to regret it someday?

A. Bamber

THE CHANGING SCENE

Morning comes, a new day dawns
The air is crisp and clear
Summer's gone but in its place
Another season's here
Autumn with its beauty
Brings a golden russet

Travelling north with hopes set high
A winding road that passes by
The Tweed with its mystery and
Villages, a resting place they lie

Idyllic surroundings full of grace
On we go still further north
Past rugged hills and dales
All nature's gifts cannot compare

Through country bathed in purple shroud
The gorse and heathers growing there
With treasured memories such as these
An Autumn day for all to share

W. K. Winfield

AUTUMN

The majestic gallows with outstretched boughs
Shudder and quake
As one by one the crisp leaves fall
In gentle winds all signs are astray

Spring is no more, its brood have flown
A new birth is due, snowdrops stand tall

Squirrels harbour their feasts
As the freshly bare elm has company again
This fine season is beseiged by beauty and grace
Were I a season, Autumn I'd be!

Shirley Cockburn

71

BORDER WINTER

Winter sunsets and twilights beckon me
to gaze at horizons
with silhouettes of leaf lost trees

Opaque windows glinting like still water ice
silver shard like scintillating diamonds
precious beyond all price

Bright moon, hazed winter blue
sky bare of cloud drips silver light over land
white, sparkling and shining proud

Secret walks through freezing nights, breathing air ice cold
o'er sparkling, twinkling, moonbeamed paths
ribbon-like, silver and gold

Billowing frigid breath hangs briefly in the air
milk white, diffuse,
vanish as if had not been there...beneath the moon bright night

Quiet night bereft of noise, save chattering teeth
bones rigid cold, flesh frost-bitten
awaits the sun's warmth to bequeath

Listen to the forming frost underfoot crackling grass
cold, more than a little forlorn
wishing for Winter to pass

Ah, Summer, were it here now...scorching heat
oh! hot bother
Again Winter sunsets, twilights, would beckon me like a
long lost brother

Ron Davis

72

STARRY NIGHT

Beneath the roof of heaven
In the frosty chasm of night
Deep-blue velvet midnight sky
Sparkles with diamond light

A milion miles beyond the moon
Though seeming ever near
Crystal stars eternal shine
A priceless chandelier

Bright eyes in our darkness
Winking to the hidden sun
Tireless watch the long night through
And gently close when dawn is won

Small is Earth when measured
Within the bounds of space
And though our world may burning fall
The stars would keep their place

Irene Wood

THE JACK FROST BITE

He creeps up so slyly and makes not a sound
Dodging the wet paving stones on the cold ground
With a flick of his fingers and a click of his heels
He covers the whole street with iced diamond weals
Beware the Jack Frost bite and the sting in his tail
For many have laughed lightly at this fairy tale

But others have known better and lived to regret
The demon from Iceland who shows no respect
Then he kisses the trees with his icicle breath
And covers their leaves in a snow white death
He leaves no mercy and only evokes fear
We pray to the Almighty...that he'll disappear

As the months go by, heat saps his strength
His knobbly iced fingers shrink in great length
The long white body is now no more than a big ball
How much have we prayed for this demon fiend to fall
No more do we fear this pathetic like lump
And give it a swift kick in his hefty white rump

Amber Nair

THE BUZZARD

Slowly and lazily broad wings flap
Effortlessly, aimlessly, deceptively
High pinned to the blue sky
Hovering
Angled wings against the wind
Folding
To plunge to earth
Roll and turn
To soar upwards again
Wing tips splayed
The big bird waits
Soaring in slow wide circles
Until first one smaller speck
A crow attacks
Then more and more
Until the Buzzard
Like a good natured dog
Slowly takes flight
Leaving the sky empty
And the silent earth below relieved

Margaret Denwood

LILY OF THE VALLEY

Delicious fragrance lingering
High over the valley
Shading from the sun beating down
So fragile
So beautiful
Alone in the unkempt soil
Oh Lily of the Valley...you give so much pleasure

Shirley Cockburn

BORDER CONFLICT

Borders Region, ancient scene
Of battles long ago
Where brave men fought and died
To beat the foe
The battle rages on
But not with swords
Men in grey suits
Mouth it with their words
They fight their fight
From comfortable position
Facing Parliamentary Opposition
Devolution is the battle of today
And Nationalistic Valour...may well pay
But are these men as brave
As who fought then
When the sword...was mightier than the pen

Alan Duggan

FLODDEN

Rank with death...was Flodden Field
Witness to a massacre of thousands
Of weary soldiers who had marched for days
Determined not to yield

The Battle began
The slaying was fast
Screams rendered the smoke filled air

Corpses lay strewn...just cannon fodder
Bludgeoned and piked
Father and son...brother wie' brother
This was their fall from lauder

The trampled earth was stained and sodden
Awash with Scottish pride
Bloodied bodies...just lying still
In a grave to remember...called Flodden

Assunta Arrighi

FORGET ME NOT

I sat and surveyed from Hadrian's wall
A landscape that cried
And dripped the blood of a thousand young men
Who like corn had been scythed

And then by a pele tower I stood amazed
As the Ettrick Shepherd walked into my gaze
And the past sang a song that I seemed to know
And my mind whispered soft "will you go lassie go"

Then all at once I was struck by a thought
Do anything but forget-me-not
The reiver in me like a wild gallowglas
Traded adventure for a humdrum face mask

I built a wall to guard my heart
Longing for love but so set apart
Don't judge me or my condition
I am not in need of a physician

The battle lost I stood amazed
As the Ettrick Shepherd walked into my gaze
I sat and surveyed from Hadrian's wall
Emotion that cried

And dropped the pain of a long lost love
Through scorn I had chosen to scythe

Francis McFall

SOMEWHERE...SOMETIME

If war be glorified, heroically storied
What of the peace...is it just caprice?
We fight for sanity as well as we can
Which is what we had...before war began

We scatter the battlefields far and wide
With the bodies of humans who fought and died
Driven by grief, their loved ones mourn
Waiting for the next war...beginning at dawn

Tom Oman

THE BATTLE

I thought of the blood that was wasted
flowing deep from each man's core
draining into the ageless soil
as longsword clashed with claymore

I thought of the hatred that each man had
both tribes thinking...the other was wrong
how instead of being willing to share the land
both claimed it as their own

I thought of how each man was a mother's son
and a family would have cried
when all their menfolk did not return
from the Border Countryside

I thought of shouts and curses
filling the air in days gone by
how life seemed so expendible
and it was acceptable to die

But now the air is silent
as we stand and feel the chill
remembering the carnage
in the Battle for Halidon Hill

Stuart Jeffrey

HAWICK – 1514

A bronze statue of an armoured youth
On a charger with Standard raised as proof

Of a victory over English marauders
Who were looting their way through the Borders

In the bustling town of Hawick it stands
A reminder of the English marauding bands

Armed with the knowledge that the death roll was high
From the Battle of Flodden Field...just one year gone by

Fighting strength on the Borders would be boys and old men
Unable to fight or defend against them

Encamped at nearby Hornshole were the English Force
When they received retaliation from these young Scottish boys

A brave ragged band of young men rode out
Showing great courage, the English did rout

Returned with the Standard of the English Force
Who had believed no opposition would come from this source

The Battle of Hornshole it came to be known
When the English Marauders were overthrown

Betty M. Varley

BORDERS REIVERS

Cold winter light drifts through ancient ruins
wind, sharp and harsh, sways leafless trees
sheep huddle close in hedgerows and headrigs
dreaming of spring and of soft summer breeze

Safe in the warmth of a welcoming fireside
letting my thoughts range through centuries gone
I conjure up Reivers bearing their plunder
tired, but exulting ride home before dawn

Great was the danger
but greater their courage
death was the penalty should they be caught

Where is this spirit now?
does it still linger?
does it still burn...in the true Border Scot?

Ana Maria Dodds

COLDINGHAM PRIORY

Oil painting by Assunta

The beautiful Hamlet of Coldingham which is situated in Eastern Berwickshire, houses one of the historical Priories in the Borders. The site of Coldingham Priory has been Holy Ground for over a thousand years. Perhaps nearer the two thousand mark as there is a Bronze Age cemetery site just a quarter of a mile away.

History dates back to c.A.D.635 where some sort of monastic house was found in the Coldingham area.

c.A.D.640 St Ebba, sister of King Oswy of Northumbria became head of this house.

Hence the reason why the adjacent fishing village acquired its name of St Abbs.

c.A.D.870 This foundation was destroyed by Danish raiders.

Hundreds of tourists who come to the area are not only impressed with the Priory with its long and complicated history but also the fact that it was visited by Mary Queen of Scots and accommodated her entourage of about a thousand in 1566.

The village itself which mainly is into farming and fishing, has one of the most beautiful coastlines to be seen.

Some of the streets remain narrow and cobbled and one can visualise and almost hear the clippity clopping of horses and carts of yester year.

COLDINGHAM PRIORY

Coldingham Priory majestic and bold
With so many memories within her hold
Still standing tall and a little aloof
Now, not so many beneath her roof

Her bells do chime on the Sabbath Day
Welcoming worshippers who come to pray
A preacher stands before her altar
Uniting the strong and those who falter

Housing once a royal Queen
Mary, Queen of Scots had seen
A fleeting stay with her band of men
A pity she never came back again

Historic tales of rape and pillage
Long forgotten in this sleepy village
The Vikings came and wreaked confusion
Bitterly resented was their intrusion

Tombstones are placed in decreed position
A loving memory – a final mission
To families gone that once had been
The thrust of life in a village scene

Assunta Arrighi

FLODDEN FIELD – Sept. 1513

The Border wars were many
Royal armies marched the coasts
Men were slain and people mourned
Claims to disputed ground foremost

Three hundred years of warfare
Ravaged the Borders, village and field
A frontier which divided two nations
Neither one prepared to yield

History tells of a terrible battle
The bloodshed, and men that were slain
Among the dead...the Scottish King
Never to reign or fight again

South of the Tweed at Coldstream
There stands a tall stone cross
A monument to the men who died
At Flodden Field...a reminder of the loss

B. M. Varley

WEE JAMIE

I see the clouds of smoke
From fires that burned the bodies
That had been killed on our bonnie moors
All our menfolk...young and old

I see our Wee Jamie
Running up the glen
To join his Da and the Laird
In battle for their beautiful Scotland

I see him still
The swirl of his tartan kilt
Swishing proudly to and fro
A broth of a lad

I used to smell the heather
Now it's just scored bracken
Little did I ken
That I'd never see my bonnie Jamie again

Alison Webb

JIM CLARK

Jim Clark pictured steering his Lotus to victory in the British Grand Prix

A local farmer from Edington Mains, Berwickshire. Jim Clark attained International fame as one of the most sucessful racing drivers of his time.

Unfortunately killed in his prime. Today his prowess as a Racing Driver is still held in high esteem among the racing fraternity and will never be forgotten.

His Trophy Room in the historic Border town of Duns is a tribute to such a great man with acolades from many of the 'greats' of the racing world who have come to pay homage to him.

ON THE DEATH OF JIM CLARK

No more the tortured tyres squeal
The roar of animated steel
And though twice Champion of the World
No more the checkered flag unfurled

No more for him the four wheel skid
The octane fumes, the starting grid
No more the promise of a dawn
On Border hillside...or Le Mans

No more the title 'King of Speed'
With hand and eye to match the need
No more the tumult of the heart
In pole position at the start

No more the banter in the pits
The dice with death, the war of wits
No spell of rural peace to steal
With panting collie at his heel

No more the joy of hopes fulfilled
The plaudits of the crowds he thrilled
And though twice Champion of the World
No more the checkered flag unfurled

Jock Dalgleish

A FISHERMAN'S LIFE

Leave the warmth of your wife's side
Rise at four, to catch the tide
Leave the harbour, perhaps with regret
Open sea beckons, shoot the net
Stow the fish deep in the hold
Keep them fresh and dark and cold

Thank the stars for the ocean wild
Providing the harvest to feed the child
Thank the stars for what you've got
Bread on the table, meat in the pot
Battle on through inclement weather
Face the forces and hardship together

Face the winds and the mountainous sea
Pray the Gods will heed your plea
Look to your mates, work as a team
Protect them from dangers, unforeseen
Land the catch back on the quay
Sail tomorrow, on the deep wild sea

Lynette Shaw McKone

MAN AND NATURE

Tae crush this flo'er below the sod
Was niver my intention
But ploughin' up this barren land
Creatin' man's dimension

We're always changin' Nature's face
Wi' barley, trees and corn
A ken what A can sei the day
But what will A sei the morn?

They pu' the hedges oot tae burn
They say it is for need
But a joost wadna be sae shair
That word should no be greed!

The sparras a' hae lost their nests
They burnt them in the fire
Sae noo they're like the swallows
An' buildin' in the byre

A workin' bee'll niver rest
It only thinks o' honey
But man in his destructive ways
Can only think o' money

Thomas Calvert

A MAN AND HIS DOG

Often I wander
Through hills and countryside
With my faithful collie dog called Ben
We would stroll so far and wide
Ben loved to chase those rabbits
The bunnies he could not abide
But they just made a fool of him
To their warrens they would hide
He thought he was superior
When he made them scatter and flee
And all he was trying to do
Was round them up for me

Then I heard a dog barking
When a spaniel came in sight
"Stay here", his master called to him
"Stay here, come back to heel
That other dog might want to fight
You can't know how he'll feel"

I asked the stranger "what's its name?"
He said, "I call him Sam
He never wanders far from me
A true friend for any man"

It's nigh on thirty years since then
And still we are great friends
Walking through the hills still yet
Long gone are Sam and Ben

New ones came to take their place
All cherished as a pet
There was Sheila and Tam
Now it's Heddie and Pam
God...give them all your grace

H. S. Paterson

92

A BOY

Who is the boy who walks alone
Through woods forests, up crooked lanes
Trailing his bag of odds and ends
Forgotten awhile his many friends

He rarely cares the way he looks
The sight of a rabbit, his rag-eared books
To him mean more, a way of life
Than disco rocker's, and daily strife

Sitting barefoot, a trickling stream
Sandwich and rod, dreaming his dream
Troubles of all sorts are left behind
A boy by himself, and an easy mind

M. H. Glencross

ALONE

I stand in a crowd alone but aware
Looking for someone with thoughts to share

A lift of the eyebrow...a smile in the eyes
Return it quickly before it dies

Do I hope for something rare?
Standing alone with hope...not despair

Olive Young

A DREAM

The children of the world
One day will unite
To ban all kinds
Of war and fight
Getting rid of all weapons
That kill and maim
Sending out a message
All saying the same

Mattering not of
Colour or creed
All equal as one
No room for greed
If only we had tried harder
Me and you
Could we have made
This dream come true?

A. Bamber

FIRST IMPRESSIONS

The reflected sun shimmers
Like an underwater light
The ragged cliff face
A patchwork of red loamy soil
And hues of different grasses
From deep emerald through to burning ochre

Seaweed splattered sand
Tumbled rocks in shapeless forms
Lie casually, anywhere
Past avalanches of boulders, reveal strata
Millions of years compressed
Into a few feet of weeping grey matter

The crumbling remains of an old sea wall
Blends naturally with its rocky neighbours
Above all, on the cliff top, in endlessly neat formation
Caravans survey the scene
A discordant strain on taut nerve ends
Like the proverbial 'lap dog' at first, my dog 'dogged me'

Now Tess explores her new territory with gusto
While I scramble over rocky mounds
And slither over slimy weeds
She flees with abandon
Across bands of seaweed
Forever exploring
Chasing the elusive seagull, cooling in the brine

My new habitat is peopled
Frighteningly different
Startlingly new
And exciting

Steph Mason

96

CHILDHOOD RECOLLECTIONS

Coldingham Hostel
Where she tied
Dusters
To their feet!

SYHA Warden
With a sense of
Fun
About work!

Two little boys
Polished all the
Floor
With gusto!

The common room
Well polished
Shone
With glee!

Happy laughter
Hilarious slidings
Along
Its length!

Border Hostel
Whose warden had
Humour
In abundance!

Grown men
Who well remember
Happy
Border Hostelling!

Mary Fawbert Wilson

DESTINY AWAITS...

What peace awaits within thy tired room
The love that blooms, craves simplicity
Your pen or quill alights with loved tranquillity
Read I your note with trembling hands I wait
Is this our love or some cruel awaited fate

I see your oil lamp aurored in the shady light
My carriage speeds I must have you...within my sight
Oh! sweet fortune smile with sheltering arms
The sweet honeysuckle cannot compete with your charms

Deep in this love box your words are locked with care
My love for you so humble, but a thought to dare
Your tender love shines amidst ribbons afire
You and I must meet...I this desire

Look up this once as I glance your way
Phantom or ghost, dry your eyes this day
When our paths meet, when this journey will break
Our love will survive when the cards have spake

Fate is our destiny for a little while
Not long our sorrow, with pitying smile
You will know my face, hidden secrets behind
When the time hands are altered...this treasure to find

June Maxwell

DAY IS DONE

Day is done, and night draws near
Dusk is settling over the fellside farms

The men come home, labours done
Faces red with setting sun

The children in their beds lay sleeping
As into the room stealthy night comes creeping

The old man sits by the kitchen fire
Puffing at his blackened briar

Remembering days of countless number
Until he too...nods in to restful slumber

R. S. Wooley

BORDERS

All of us build borders
We create checkpoints
Demand passports
And ask that the visitor
State their business in our personal space

All of us build borders
Keep ourselves to ourselves
Drown in bureaucracy
Offer red tape as an excuse
But imagine that the other man's grass is greater

All of us build borders
Then we invade our next door neighbour
Only to retreat
And take an even more insular stance
Adapting our language to suit our sulk

All of us build borders
Then sign non-aggression pacts
Offer slogans without facts
In an attempt to have a lasting peace
Which will save face

Well I thank God love knows no limit
Like a child in innocence it pulls checkpoints down
I thank God that love sees no borders
And love will break your heart to be found

David Isaac

CHILDHOOD

On sunny days we'd walk about
or ask to take a bairn out

then to the park we all would go
the flowers there made such a show

with bottles of water
and our bread wie jam

we'd whoop and hollar
and laugh as we ran

fishing rods and jam jars
tied atop with string

to catch the minnows and tadpoles
and then to plop them in

see if you like butter
or make a daisy chain

shout and wave as you espy
the lass from up the lane

rosy cheeked and tired
as homeward bound you go

we had such a smashing time back then
or tell me...didn't you know

Irene Davis

THE BOAT HOUSE

This fishing shiel was a haven to me
When I was growing up
My father taught me to row...and not be afraid of the sea

The peace, the tranquillity a welcome diversion
From turbulent times which were a plenty
In this wooden hut I found no coercion

My father's wisdom I can recall
His love and humanity a lesson to me
He was a very special man...respected by all

Then all too soon I became a man
With pressures by the store
I left my homeland where first it all began

City life was not for me, the smoke, the pace, the bad
Father now dead...a great sadness reigns
You can't replace a Dad

My wild oats were sown
A frustration expelled
From the terrible anger of which it had grown

The wheel has now turned it's my turn to be
Back to my roots and the fishing shiel
Now my sons shall learn...not to be afraid of the sea

Anthony Hyslop

A CUMBRIAN GENT

He listens to the birds singing and watches rabbits run
He wonders what the day will bring in the way of fun
He used to work down the pits, but now he's old and grey
Well past his 'best buy' date...many folk would say

But this grand Gent has many a tale to tell everyone
About the harsh, but good old days that have been and gone
His memory is crystal clear although his body frail
His blue eyes laugh and sparkle when offered a glass of ale

He'll only have a couple though...taking's not his way
Because you must remember...tomorrow is another day
He's eighty now and may not have many more days left
And when he finally does go...the town will be bereft

He's always been there you see, keeping a watchful eye
To help the young ones stay in line 'old worlde style'
Yes he's a Gent of Cumbria...loved and not abused
Unlike a lot of pensioners, you hear of in the news!

P.A.F.

A FISH SONNET

Thar in the deid watter ahent the brig
Atween the caul-brat and the flew portelis
A sneip reid siluar schuil o sea troutis lig
Hingand, a bab o weet blak bakkit schellis
Up frae the dirk lowne stell alow the caul

A fresch rin trout loups heich intae the gait
Gallus tae fecht the ramstam fisch-gang maul
His braissant breenge is styntit be the spate
The fisch forfain assayis tae jyne the lave

Brekand in a blink the braisit menyie
Intae the freithie steir, thrawn ilkane gaes
Aince mair besynes they tak thar stance fischie
And sae suld we, hing bak frae warsle says
Hainand our stentit strinth for ither days

Tony Paterson

"IF ONLY"

Shock horror
It's happened again
What has?
This has!
Every time I sit down to write
All I can see
are...
Old men
With sagging skin
Lived-in eyes
Cobweb wives
Never smile
Only stare
Ashes to ashes
Nothing there
Just a grave
Of yesterday
Dust to dust
I hear them say
Life lived
So complete
Sad regret
Bittersweet
Hearts cry
To be free
I am scared
They are me!
Dawn breaks
Upon this shore
I won't say
"IF ONLY"
Anymore

David Isaac

TRAGEDY

Coniston Water its depths are a grave
To a man called Campbell
Who was young and brave

On a damp cold day his life was cut short
On his final run he tried to abort
When suddenly his craft took flight
To see it break up was an awesome sight

To this day his record's the best
But the depths of Coniston
Is where he's laid to rest

Shaun McDowell

THE BORDERS SAILOR

We hear a lot today
Of what our Statesmen have to say
About the future of the present generation
Of the homes that will be ours, with their gardens and flowers
And children with a better education

I'm just a stoker aboard a ship
Making yet another trip
My quarters, little better than a hovel
And nearly all the time
I am below the waterline
My uniform...a sweat rag and a shovel

Hear us now, you ruling classes
We, the Merchant Navy crew
We want no fancy medals or ribbons red and blue
All we want from this old country
That means...you and you and you
Is something more substantial...A sincere I Owe You!

J. F. Bryden

(Written on the Murmansk run during the Second World War)

IF I SHOULD WALK THIS WAY AGAIN

If I should walk this way again,
If I should pass this lane,
Then again I will remember
You wave a sad farewell to me.

If God permits me to come home
From the hell where I now roam,
The first thing I wish to see
Is you awaiting, watching for me.

If fate decides that I must die
In this trench where I now lie,
I'll remember the love we had
And die a happy soldier lad.

But if luck holds – as well it could,
(As we've hoped and prayed it would)
Then I'll return home again
And take you as my bride.

Loui

Oil painting by Assunta

THE VIXEN

Hunting and hunted, trapped and run to ground
With cunning wiles and swiftness without sound
Secures a place in nature's canopy
And we of human kind admire, her style and her segacity

On urban land she wanders now
As rural plains contract
Denying space but showing how
She still insists her here and now

While man debates with arrogance of mind
Should she continue to be free and live at will
Or should it be by means of man made villainy
He would be denied her lovely symphony

Eliza Farrant

111

MIDSUMMER NIGHT

My down to earth friend Diedre
Says it was nicked from the cemetery
But my little stone girl by the trellis
I have christened Edith Alice

She lifted her skirt so neat
As I linger longer on the seat
Beside her, my mind at peace

It was in an old junk yard
Behind a smashed flower vase
I found this maid of grace
Small dancing feet, sweet face

But in the middle of the night
I got quite a fright
When I got up for the loo

'Cos Edith Alice had moved!
I ventured down the garden, felt my arteries harden
For there was this daisy chain on the seat
With two small stone slippers from tired dancing feet!

Catherine Nair

THE BALLAD OF LORD PATRICK AND
THE MILLER'S DAUGHTER

Oh Father dear, I am ashamed
For I have been betrayed
The old Earl's son has spoken me fair
And I am no more a maid

See where this hour Lord Patrick comes
Upon his steed so white
I know he rides to a lady fair
Whom he shall wed tonight

My Lord, you make your marriage here
Nor set my daughter by
Or I will strike you a desperate blow
And you a dead man lie

I cannot wed your daughter dear
Though true I have clipped her round
For I must marry for gold and lands
And love where these are found

Out of my way! Or my bounding steed
Shall shoulder you aside!
The miller has gone to the swift mill-race
To turn the mill-wheel wide

The water freed, has covered with speed
The way which the 'groom must pass
No road he finds, but a rising flood
Where he looked for the young green grass

Now swim my steed, as you have never swam
To bring me safe to shore
And a silver harness you shall wear
If I live this day or more

No bridle bells will Lord Patrick hear
No lady fair will he wed
For the water has drowned his bonny white steed
And he lies in his saddle...dead

Beth Harris

113

THE LINE

The line must be defined
If place is to be found
Equator heat or frozen mass
Tells much about our ground

Static feet don't hide the line
Defines just where we stand
The body and the mind...so blind
To feel and see the hinterland

Excrescences in abundance found
Flaw all matter of mankind
Yes, even genius is holed
By power from nature's clear design

Earthly chains secure the limbs
Within the spherical complexity
Longitude and lattitude cojoin
While oceans close their entity

The voice of human dignity pervades
To tell of wisdom now man-made

Douglas Haig Griffiths

114

LOVE IS...

Being without you
Leaving me empty and hollow
Like a sky without clouds, sun or moon

With you I was someone...a special person
When you left
You took something I thought was mine

What you gave me
Was something new to live with
An eternal waiting...that hurts inside

But knowing
That you are with someone else
Is...hurting me even more

Michelle Amanda Whiteley

COMING HOME

I came into the Borderlands
That from a child I dreamed of
So much was offered to my mind
I always wondered what I'd find

I travelled all around the world
To places of great beauty
Somewhere stamped in history
And others told a story

Now the day had come for me
To make the journey northbound
The choice was now within my mind
Where I would settle down

Ann R. Ferguson

THE BORDERS

What can I say about them?
A city slicker like me
The Borders are where people part

And with one footstep
Are out of Scotland
And into England...a foreign land

Yet...as we stand on the threshold
Do we not see ghosts
Of warriors long gone

Roman legions with lance and shield
Proud soldiers in tartan plaid
Redcoats with muskets at the ready

Each transparent face telling its tale
Of victory or surrender
History has been thrust upon the Borders

Where beauty of the land is but a fleeting glance
I think too of Sir Walter Scott
A Borders man

Painting pictures
With tales of intrigue
Of his beloved land

The Borders for me is an invisible but cultural line
Between 'them' and 'us'
Let us guard the Borders well

Ina McCaig

LOVE...IS

To walk again with the one I love
Hand in hand by the river dove

carpets of grass beneath my feet
Tiny hillock for a seat

Sky of blue above
Come...walk with me again my love!

Hilary Manester